Weirdest Looking
Cats & Kittens

Billy Grinslott & Kinsey Marie Books
ISBN - 9781960612823

Devon Rex cats are known for being curious, playful, and mischievous. It should come as little surprise that these cats enjoy jumping up to the highest point in a room or on your shoulder. The Devon cat is happiest when they are around others. They are social animals and do not always enjoy being left home alone, especially for a long time. Devon Rex cats are intelligent. They can learn many of the same tricks and commands people typically teach dogs.

Curious and clown-like, the Cornish Rex cat thrives on entertaining people. This cat has kitten-like energy well into adulthood. They like to play and love to be picked up and handled or cuddled with. Their short coat is ideal because of low shedding and minimal grooming. Their fur comes in more than 40 different colors and patterns.

The Scottish Fold got its name because its ears lay flat. They are born with straight ears. The fold begins to develop when the kitten is between 18 and 24 days old, but only if they have the gene that is responsible for the fold. Scottish folds are known for their sweet personalities and fun quirks. Oftentimes, they will sit up like people to improve their vantage point when they hear a noise. One downfall is their tail does not flex like other cats. You will have to be careful when handling them so you don't hurt their tail.

A Bengal cats coat features spots, rosettes, and marbling, giving them an exotic, jungle cat appearance. In fact, the Bengal is the only domestic cat breed with rosette markings. These cats are highly active and almost always on the move. Bengal cats love to play with people and will vocalize their desire to interact with you. Bengal cats love to play in the water. It's not unusual for a Bengal cat to join his owner in the shower.

Manx cats have long back legs and can jump extraordinarily high. They can jump 4 feet high from a standing position. Their long back legs also make them extremely fast runners. One other feature you will notice is they have no tail or a very short tail. They typically have an arched back. They come in a variety of different colors. Many Manx cats suffer from a variety of painful symptoms that are collectively referred to as Manx Syndrome, including spina bifida.

Sphynx cats don't look like cats, and they resemble moles. Sphynx might be hairless cats, but they are full of love and affection. Owners will tell you that Sphynx cats have a friendly nature. They love their owners and generally get along with dogs and other cats. If you are looking for a loving cat companion, they make an excellent choice. This cat can get cold quickly since they have no fur to protect them from cold. It's better to keep them indoors.

The Japanese Bobtail cat has a short tail. Their tail is more like a rabbit's tail than that of other cats. The tails on these cats are all unique, and no two are alike. They can also have two different colored eyes. The Japanese Bobtail is an active, sweet, loving and intelligent cat. They love to be with people and will play endlessly. They learn their name and respond to it. They bring toys to people and play fetch with a favorite toy for hours.

the Abyssinian is not a lethargic lap cat. These highly active cats are always on the move. Their athleticism and curiosity result in a breed that is constantly jumping, climbing, and exploring. The Abyssinian has cougar-like appearance, thanks to its ticked coat. It's a coat has individual strands that alternate bands of color. Abys love to interact with people. They have a dog-like attachment to their owners and prefer to be an involved member of the family.

Ocicats are among the breeds of cats who enjoy water and may try to join you in the shower or bathtub. This cat won't turn down an invitation to ride in cars or travel with you. They are incredibly athletic and can jump to high spots, balance on narrow ledges, and get to places other cats probably wouldn't think of. This cat enjoys a lot of attention and very able to demand it when they need it.

Exotics Shorthairs are sometimes born with long hair. Exotics Shorthairs are not jumpers or sprinters, although they still like to run around in the house. The Exotic Shorthair is as low maintenance and laid back. This kitty has a double layer coat, with a thick, downy under layer that lifts the topcoat away from the body. With their adorable, teddy bear appearance, the Exotic Shorthair is regularly featured in movies. They are the second most popular cat in the US. They make an all around good pet in many ways.

Siamese kittens are born a creamy white color. Their darker color patterns develop later. Most cats are known for their sharp acute vision, especially at night. But Siamese cats have a genetic flaw that makes it difficult for them to see color and distinguish details at night. Their eyes will look crossed because of this. Siamese cats are social, they are very friendly. They are a great cuddly companion. They are great for families with dogs and small children.

The American Bobtail cat has a stubby tail like a bobcat. American Bobtails are fascinated by shiny objects. This means that you should be careful of where you leave your jewelry or loose change, they may take it. These cats are like Houdini the magician. They have been known to escape from closed rooms and open doors. These cats are outgoing, empathetic, and they make for excellent companions. They are playful, friendly, and intelligent. They like spending time with their family, they get along with dogs, and other cats.

The Selkirk Rex is an interesting cat breed, easily recognized by their long curly coat. These cats developed their curls through a natural genetic mutation. Everything about this cat is curly, even its whiskers. The Selkirk rex is the only breed of cat named for a real person. Some Selkirk's get dirty easily, so it's recommended to keep up with routine baths to keep them clean. A Selkirk is active, yet still affectionate, and does well in a home with children as well as other pets.

The oriental shorthair has unusual looks. The Oriental Shorthair is thought to be one of the most intelligent cats, if not the most intelligent. They are highly trainable because they are very curious, and they love interaction and stimulation. They get attached to people, very quickly. Oriental Shorthairs are ready to bond with their family. it's not unusual for an Oriental shorthair to live more than 15 years. Oriental Shorthair breed is known for its honking sounds, a few cats only make this sound when feeling frustrated or upset.

The Toyger cat got its name because it has tiger like stripes. Toyger cats have shorter legs than other breeds, which is a common trait of big cats. They also have long toes and big paws like big cats. They have a positive personality, such as a pleasant temperament, relaxed personality, intelligence, trainability, and ease of handling. They are content to live with people, including children. They make good pets.

The American Curl cat got its name because its ears curl. American curl cats are born with straight ears. They begin to curl in three to five days' time, and they settle into their fully curled shape within about four months. They are nicknamed the Peter Pan of cats because of their playful, kitten like personalities. It's important to always handle American curl ears with care, to not damage their ear cartilage.

The Pixie-bob cat has a short tail and looks more like a wild cat. They were specifically bred to resemble the North American Bobcat. They are very rare. They enjoy playing and splashing around in the water, a trait that sets them apart from other cats. The Pixie-bob is described has a dog-like personality. These cats can be leash-trained easily and love to take walks with people. These cats are highly intelligent and have a natural curiosity. They love exploring and searching for things.

The Ragdoll was given its name because of the cat's tendency to go limp when lifted, just like a rag doll. They are one of the largest breeds of domestic cats. When Ragdolls are born, they are pure white and develop their coat color and pattern over the first 2 weeks of their life. They love to play and sometimes enjoy a game of fetch. They are often known as puppy-like as they follow people around and they are very loyal. Just like dogs, a Ragdoll cat will often greet you when you come home.

The Lambkin cat has short legs. They got their name because their coat resembles that of a lamb. While Lambkins are smaller and have shorter legs than most other cat breeds, their head is the same size as an average-sized cat. The Lambkin cat is a cross between the dwarf Munchkin cat and curly-haired Selkirk Rex. The Lambkins are often considered as one of the tiniest cat breeds that exist today and weigh from 4 to 9 pounds.

The Munchkin cat is one of the smallest cats with short legs. Munchkin cats come in all types of colors and patterns. These cats make great indoor pets and get along good with other cats and dogs. The size of their legs does not affect the speed and agility of the Munchkin cat. They are high energy and possess extraordinary speed. Munchkin cats like to hoard things that are shiny. They are known to steal, hide, and hoard shiny objects. Better hide your jewelry, coins, and keys. They also like to sit like a person on their back feet or will even stand up.

The Teacup kitten got its name because its small enough to sit in a teacup. Teacup kittens will not grow no matter what or how much you feed them. They will have the same tiny size even in their adulthood. They grow to about six inches, with many being smaller. They are about two-thirds smaller in size when compared to the size of the normal adult cat. Some are naturally cute, while others may look undernourished and have a stunted appearance.

LaPerm cats got their name because they have long curly fur. But, they are low maintenance. Their coat comes in different lengths and colors. LaPerm cats originated from farm cats. They are affectionate, funny, smart, and playful. LaPerm's are known for being highly affectionate, adaptable, and energetic.

Peterbald cats can be hairless, making them look weird. Peterbald's have a very fast metabolism and need more food than average cats. This is due to trying to stay warm, because they don't have fur to keep them warm. This unusual cat has many distinct features, including huge ears and webbed toes. Peterbald's are friendly, sweet-tempered, and incredibly rare cats. They make loyal pets and form deep attachments to their people.

Ly koi cats resemble little werewolves thanks to their sparse coats and distinctive furless facial masks. A genetic mutation is responsible for giving Ly koi cats their distinctive looks. Because most Ly koi cats have either sparse or no fur, they should be kept indoors. They shed fur a couple times a year, just like dogs.

Ukrainian Levkoy cats can have straight ears or ears that are rounded and curled down. They are for the most part hairless. They sometimes have curly whiskers and long tails with pointy ends. Levkoys are very sociable, enjoying family company as well as the company of other domestic pets. They are friendly, playful, and intelligent cats.

Donskoy cats are also hairless and can have striking blue eyes. The Donskoy cat is extremely social. The Donskoy cat is very intriguing and inquisitive and soft-hearted. These friendly, active cats are known for being very loyal. In fact, their loyalty is often compared to that of dogs. Donskoy cats are typically active, they require sufficient stimulation to keep them entertained.

The Highlander cat has rounded ears and features fur colors and patterns compared to wild cats. They are a very muscular cat. They also have a short tail like a bobcat. Despite the big cat look, the Highlander is a human-oriented, friendly, playful cat, very active and confident. Highlander cats often seek out and enjoy playing in water. They also have more toes than an average cat.

Savannah cats are a mix of wild serval cats and domestic cats. Savannah cats are cousins to the lynx and ocelot, and they all wear the same spotted coat. Savannah cats love water. It is not unusual to find them swimming around, splashing and having the time of their life. The Savannah cat is an active, adventurous, and curious cat. The Savannah quickly creates strong bonds to with their owners and follow them around just like a dog.

Egyptian Mau cats originated in Egypt and that's how they got their name. They are one of the only cats to have light fur with cheetah like markings. The Egyptian Mau is the only natural spotted cat breed. Egyptian Maus are the fastest of all domestic cats, capable of reaching speeds of 30 miles per hour. They are capable of leaping six feet in the air from a standing position. They have musical voices. They chirp, chortle, and make unusual sounds when petted.

Janus cats have a history of being born with two heads. They got their name from the roman god named Janus who was portrayed as having two faces. Janus cats can have a variety of health problems due to their deformity. Common problems could involve issues with eating, respiration, and even proper brain activity. They don't tend to live very long.

The calico cat can have a variety of different colors and piercing yellow eyes. They typically have three colors and that is what calico stands for. The typical calico cat has large patches of white with smaller patches of orange and black. Calico cats have been thought to be especially lucky because they are so rare. Japanese sailors would travel with Calico cats onboard their ships for protection, because they thought they brought them good luck. Male calico cats are very rare due to genetic defects.

The Chimera cat is known for having a half black face and front upper body. What's weird is the black on their face and upper body can be on the opposite side. They can also have two different colored eyes. Most are sweet and gentle, but they can have an independent and confident side to them. They are just as lovable and wonderful as any other kitty.

Khao Manee cats usually have 2 different colored eyes. These cats are related to the Siamese breed, which means you can expect them to be on the vocal side. Some people consider the Khao Manee cat to be good luck. Curious, intelligent and people oriented, the Khao Manee is a friendly and affectionate companion. The Khao Manee is an athletic cat with an active, playful temperament.

The Elf cat has ears that look like an elf and that's how it got its name. They also can have different colored eyes. They can also be hairless. The Elf cat is a hybrid created by breeding the American Curl and the Sphynx. They are very kind, affectionate and gentle. They adapt well to living in a multi-pet household, especially since there will always be someone for them to play with.

The chinchilla Persian cat can have large eyes and an underbite where its lower teeth stick out of its mouth. Despite their weird looks, they have a very quiet and gentle nature, and they make great pets for some people. They don't tolerate small children very well. These cats form close bonds with their owners and they become very attached to them.

The Minskin is a small, stocky cat with a round head, semi-stocky body, and short legs. It looks hairless but it has short hair that grows on the face, ears, legs, and tail. It is still a weird looking cat with its odd, shaped head and big ears. Minskins appear to be bald on the neck, chest, and belly, but these areas are covered with a very soft, downy fur.

Author Page

Billy Grinslott & Kinsey Marie Books

Copyright, All Rights Reserved

ISBN - 9781960612823

www.ingramcontent.com/pod-product-compliance
Lightning Source LLC
Chambersburg PA
CBHW041537040426
42446CB00002B/123